THE LANGUAGE M
ARCHITECT

TURNING DATA INTO INTELLIGENCE WITH PYTHON

OLIVER LUCAS JR

Preface
The Language Model Architect: Turning Data into Intelligence with Python

In the heart of the digital age, we're witnessing a revolution driven by artificial intelligence. Language models, once a distant dream, have become a reality, reshaping industries and redefining human-computer interaction. This book is your guide to understanding and harnessing the power of these remarkable tools.

Through the lens of Python, a versatile and powerful programming language, we'll explore the intricacies of language models, from their fundamental concepts to cutting-edge applications. You'll learn how to build, train, and deploy language models that can generate creative text, translate languages, answer complex questions, and much more.

This book is designed for both beginners and experienced programmers. Whether you're a curious learner or a seasoned data scientist, you'll find valuable insights and practical guidance. We'll delve into the theoretical foundations, practical implementations, and ethical considerations of language model development.

As you embark on this journey, remember that the future of AI is bright, and language models are at the forefront of this exciting frontier. By mastering the art of language model architecture, you'll be equipped to shape the future of technology and human interaction.

Let's begin this exciting exploration together!

TABLE OF CONTENTS

Chapter 4

4.1 The Transformer Architecture Explained

4.2 Attention Mechanism: The Heart of Transformers

4.3 Implementing Transformers with Hugging Face

Chapter 5

5.1 Transfer Learning for Language Models

5.2 Fine-Tuning for Text Generation

5.3 Fine-Tuning for Text Classification

Chapter 6

6.1 Generating Text with Language Models

6.2 Controlling Text Generation: Temperature, Top-k, and Top-p Sampling

6.3 Creative Text Generation: Poetry, Code, and Scripts

Chapter 7

Chapter 8

Chapter 9

Chapter 10

10.1 Bias and Fairness in Language Models

10.2 Privacy and Security Concerns in Language Models

10.3 Responsible AI Practices

Chapter 1

Introduction to Language Models

1.1 Language Models: A Brief Overview

A language model is a type of artificial intelligence that is designed to understand and generate human language. It's like a computer program that has learned the rules of grammar, syntax, and semantics of a language. By processing vast amounts of text data, these models can predict the next word in a sentence, generate text, translate languages, and even answer complex questions.

How Do Language Models Work?

Language models are trained on massive datasets of text and code. As they process this data, they learn patterns and relationships between words and sentences. This allows them to make predictions about the likelihood of a particular word or phrase appearing in a given context.

Types of Language Models

There are several types of language models, each with its own strengths and weaknesses:

1 Statistical Language Models:

Rely on statistical techniques to analyze large amounts of text data.

They calculate the probability of a word sequence based on its historical occurrence.

2 Neural Network Language Models:

Utilize neural networks to learn complex patterns in language data.

They are capable of capturing intricate semantic and syntactic relationships.[1]

3 Transformer-Based Language Models:

A powerful type of neural network architecture that has revolutionized natural language processing.

Transformers excel at handling long-range dependencies and capturing contextual information.

Applications of Language Models

Language models have a wide range of applications, including:

Natural Language Processing (NLP):

Text generation

Machine translation

Text summarization

Sentiment analysis

Question answering

Code Generation:

Autocompleting code

Generating code snippets

Chatbots and Virtual Assistants:

Providing informative and engaging conversations

As language models continue to evolve, we can expect to see even more innovative and powerful applications emerge.

1.2 History of Language models

A Brief History of Language Models

The journey of language models has been a fascinating one, marked by significant advancements over the decades. Here's a brief overview:

Early Beginnings: Statistical Language Models

1980s: The foundation of statistical language models was laid.These models relied on statistical techniques to analyze large amounts of text data and predict the likelihood of a word sequence.

N-gram Models: A popular technique where the probability of a word is estimated based on the n-1 preceding words.

Neural Network Revolution

1990s: Neural networks, particularly Recurrent Neural Networks (RNNs), were introduced. These models could process sequential data, making them suitable for language tasks.

Long Short-Term Memory (LSTM) Networks: A type of RNN capable of capturing long-term dependencies, which improved the performance of language models.

The Rise of Transformers

2017: The Transformer architecture emerged, revolutionizing the field of natural language processing.

Attention Mechanism: A key component of Transformers, allowing the model to focus on relevant parts of the input sequence.

BERT and GPT-3: Large language models based on the Transformer architecture, capable of generating human-quality text, translating languages, and answering complex questions.

The Present and Future

Continued Innovation: Researchers are continually pushing the boundaries of language model capabilities.

Real-world Applications: Language models are being integrated into various applications, such as chatbots, virtual assistants, and content generation tools.

Ethical Considerations: As language models become more powerful, it's crucial to address ethical concerns like bias, misinformation, and privacy.

The future of language models is promising, with the potential to transform industries and revolutionize human-computer interaction.

1.3 The Role of Python in Language Model Development

Python's Role in Language Model Development

Python has become the de facto language for language model development due to its simplicity, versatility, and a rich ecosystem of libraries and frameworks. Here's how Python contributes to this field:

1. Readability and Productivity:

Simple Syntax: Python's clear and concise syntax allows developers to focus on the core concepts of language models rather than complex language syntax.

Rapid Prototyping: Its interactive nature enables quick experimentation and iteration, accelerating the development process.

2. Powerful Libraries and Frameworks:

TensorFlow and PyTorch: These deep learning frameworks provide the building blocks for creating sophisticated neural networks, including those used in language models.

NumPy and SciPy: These libraries offer efficient numerical computations, essential for handling large datasets and performing complex mathematical operations.

Scikit-learn: This machine learning library provides tools for preprocessing data, feature engineering, and model evaluation, which are crucial steps in language model development.

Hugging Face Transformers: This library simplifies the process of working with pre-trained language models, allowing developers to fine-tune them for specific tasks.

3. Strong Community and Resources:

Large and Active Community: Python's vibrant community provides extensive support, documentation, and tutorials.

Open-Source Libraries: A wealth of open-source libraries and frameworks are available, accelerating development and fostering collaboration.

Online Resources: Numerous online courses, tutorials, and forums offer learning opportunities and problem-solving assistance.

4. Integration with Other Tools:

Seamless Integration: Python can be easily integrated with other tools and technologies, such as cloud platforms (AWS, GCP, Azure), databases, and visualization tools.

Data Processing and Analysis: Python excels at handling large datasets, cleaning, preprocessing, and analyzing data, which is crucial for training language models.

By leveraging Python's strengths, researchers and developers can efficiently build and deploy state-of-the-art language models that push the boundaries of artificial intelligence.

Chapter 2

Fundamentals of Natural Language Processing (NLP)

2.1 Text Preprocessing Techniques

Text preprocessing is a crucial step in natural language processing (NLP) that involves cleaning and transforming raw text data into a format suitable for analysis[1] or modeling. It helps improve the quality and accuracy of NLP tasks like sentiment analysis, text classification, and machine translation.

Here are some common text preprocessing techniques:

1. Lowercasing:

Converts all text to lowercase to standardize the text and reduce the vocabulary size.

2. Removing Punctuation and Special Characters:

Eliminates punctuation marks, numbers, and other special characters that might not be relevant to the analysis.

3. Removing Stop Words:

Removes common words like "the," "and," "is," that have little semantic meaning and can add noise to the data.

4. Tokenization:

Breaks down text into individual words or tokens, which are the basic units of analysis.

5. Stemming and Lemmatization:

Reduces words to their root form:

Stemming: Chops off suffixes to get the root form (e.g., "running" -> "run").

Lemmatization: Uses morphological analysis to derive the base form of a word (e.g., "better" -> "good").

6. Part-of-Speech Tagging:

Assigns grammatical tags to each word, such as noun, verb, adjective, etc., to understand the word's role in the sentence.

7. Named Entity Recognition (NER):

Identifies and classifies named entities like persons, organizations, locations, and dates within the text.

8. Text Normalization:

Converts text into a standardized format, such as converting numbers to words or expanding contractions.

9. Handling Contractions:

Expands contractions like "can't" to "cannot" to improve text representation.

10. Handling Emojis and Emoticons:

Converts emojis and emoticons into text or removes them, depending on the specific task.

By applying these techniques, you can clean and prepare text data for further analysis and modeling, leading to more accurate and meaningful insights.

2.2 Text Representation: Word Embeddings and Transformers

Text representation is a fundamental task in natural language processing (NLP) that involves converting text into numerical representations that can be understood by machine learning models.

Word Embeddings

Word embeddings are a technique for representing words as dense vectors of real numbers. Each dimension of the vector captures semantic and syntactic information about the word.

Types of Word Embeddings:

Word2Vec: This technique trains a neural network to predict the context of a word given its surrounding words or vice versa.

GloVe: This technique combines global word-word co-occurrence statistics with local context information.

FastText: This technique represents words as the sum of character-level n-gram embeddings, which is useful for handling out-of-vocabulary words.

Transformers

Transformer models have revolutionized the field of NLP, surpassing traditional RNN-based models. They leverage a mechanism called **self-attention** to weigh the importance of different parts of the input sequence.

Key Components of a Transformer:

Encoder: Processes the input sequence and generates contextual representations for each token.

Decoder: Generates the output sequence, conditioned on the encoder's output and its own previous outputs.

Self-Attention: Allows the model to weigh the importance of different parts of the input sequence when processing a specific token.

Positional Encoding: Incorporates information about the relative or absolute position of tokens in the sequence.

Popular Transformer-Based Models:

BERT (Bidirectional Encoder Representations from Transformers): A powerful model that can be fine-tuned for various NLP tasks, including text classification, question answering, and text generation.

GPT-3 (Generative Pre-trained Transformer 3): A large language model capable of generating human-quality text, translating languages, and writing different kinds of creative content.

By understanding these text representation techniques, we can effectively train and deploy advanced language models for various NLP applications.

2.3 Text Classification and Sentiment Analysis

Text Classification and Sentiment Analysis

Text classification and sentiment analysis are two important applications of natural language processing (NLP) that rely on effective text representation and machine learning techniques.

Text Classification

Text classification involves categorizing text documents into predefined classes or categories. For example, you might want to classify emails as spam or not spam, news articles by topic, or customer reviews as positive or negative.

Common Techniques for Text Classification:

Naive Bayes: A probabilistic classifier that assumes the independence of features.

Support Vector Machines (SVM): A powerful classification algorithm that finds the optimal hyperplane to separate different classes.

Decision Trees: A tree-based model that makes decisions based on a series of rules.

Random Forest: An ensemble method that combines multiple decision trees to improve accuracy.

Neural Networks: Deep learning models that can learn complex patterns in text data.

Sentiment Analysis

Sentiment analysis, a specific type of text classification, focuses on identifying and categorizing opinions expressed in text. It can be used to analyze customer reviews, social media posts, or news articles to gauge overall sentiment.

Common Techniques for Sentiment Analysis:

Machine Learning-Based Approaches: Similar to text classification, machine learning algorithms can be used to classify text as positive, negative, or neutral.

Lexicon-Based Approaches: These methods rely on sentiment lexicons, which are dictionaries of words and their associated sentiment scores.

Hybrid Approaches: Combine machine learning and lexicon-based methods to improve accuracy.

Example: Suppose you have a dataset of customer reviews for a product. You can use a sentiment analysis model to classify each review as positive, negative, or neutral. This information can be used to identify areas for improvement in the product or customer service.

Chapter 3

Building a Basic Language Model

3.1 Data Collection and Preparation

Data collection and preparation are crucial initial steps in any machine learning project, including language model development. The quality and quantity of data directly impact the performance of the model.

Data Collection

Web Scraping:

Beautiful Soup: A Python library for parsing HTML and XML documents.

Scrapy: A powerful framework for building large-scale web crawlers.

API Access:

Using APIs provided by platforms like Twitter, Reddit, or news organizations to access structured data.

Public Datasets:

Utilizing publicly available datasets like Common Crawl, Wikipedia, or datasets from academic institutions.

Creating Synthetic Data:

Generating artificial text data using techniques like text generation models or rule-based systems.

Data Preparation

Once the data is collected, it needs to be preprocessed to make it suitable for machine learning models:

Cleaning:

Removing noise, such as HTML tags, extra whitespace, and special characters.

Handling missing values: Imputing missing values or removing records with missing data.

Tokenization:

Breaking down text into individual words or tokens.

Lowercasing:

Converting text to lowercase to reduce vocabulary size.

Stop Word Removal:

Removing common words like "the," "and," "is" that have little semantic meaning.

Stemming and Lemmatization:

Reducing words to their root form to reduce vocabulary size and improve accuracy.

Part-of-Speech Tagging:

Assigning grammatical tags to words to understand their role in the sentence.

Named Entity Recognition:

Identifying and classifying named entities like persons, organizations, and locations.

Data Splitting:

Dividing the dataset into training, validation, and testing sets to evaluate model performance.

By carefully collecting and preparing data, you can ensure that your language model is trained on high-quality data and achieves optimal performance.

3.2 Training a Recurrent Neural Network (RNN)

Recurrent Neural Networks (RNNs) are a type of artificial neural network designed to process sequential data, making them well-suited for language modeling tasks.

Key Steps in Training an RNN:

Data Preparation:

Tokenization: Break down text into individual words or tokens.

Numerical Representation: Convert tokens into numerical representations, such as one-hot encoding or word embeddings.

Data Splitting: Divide the dataset into training, validation, and testing sets.

Model Architecture:

RNN Cell: The basic building block of an RNN. It takes an input at time step t, the previous hidden state, and produces an output and a new hidden state.

Layers: Stack multiple RNN layers to capture complex patterns.

Loss Function: Measures the difference between the model's predicted output and the actual output. Common loss functions include cross-entropy loss.

Optimizer: Adjusts the model's parameters to minimize the loss function (e.g., Adam, SGD).

Training Process:

Forward Pass:

Input the first token into the RNN cell.

Calculate the output and the new hidden state.

Feed the new hidden state and the next token into the cell.

Repeat until the end of the sequence.

Backward Pass (Backpropagation):

Calculate the gradient of the loss function with respect to the model's parameters.

Update the parameters using the optimizer.

Iterate: Repeat the forward and backward passes for multiple epochs until the model converges.

Challenges and Improvements:

Vanishing Gradient Problem: As information flows through multiple layers, gradients can become very small, hindering learning.

Long-Term Dependencies: RNNs struggle to capture long-range dependencies in sequences.

To address these challenges, more advanced RNN architectures have been developed:

Long Short-Term Memory (LSTM): Uses gates to control the flow of information, allowing it to remember information for longer periods.

Gated Recurrent Unit (GRU): A simpler variant of LSTM that combines the forget and input gates into a single update gate.

By understanding the fundamentals of RNNs and addressing their limitations, you can effectively train language models for various tasks, such as text generation, machine translation, and sentiment analysis.

3.3 Evaluating Model Performance

Evaluating the performance of a language model is crucial to assess its accuracy and effectiveness. Various metrics can be used to evaluate different aspects of the model's output.

Common Evaluation Metrics:

For Text Classification:

Accuracy: The proportion of correctly classified instances.

Precision: The proportion of positive predictions that are actually positive.

Recall: The proportion of actual positive instances that are correctly identified as positive.

F1-score: The harmonic mean of precision and recall, providing a balanced measure.

Confusion Matrix: A table that summarizes the performance of a classification model on a test set.

For Text Generation:

Perplexity: Measures how well a model predicts a sequence of words. Lower perplexity indicates better performance.

BLEU (Bilingual Evaluation Understudy): Compares generated text to reference translations.

ROUGE (Recall-Oriented Understudy for Gisting Evaluation): Evaluates the quality of summaries by comparing them to reference summaries.

METEOR (Metric for Evaluation of Translation with Explicit Ordering): Considers word-level matching, stemming, and synonymy.

For Question Answering:

Exact Match: Measures the percentage of questions answered exactly correctly.

F1-score: Evaluates the precision and recall of the model's answers.

EM Score: Measures the exact match accuracy.

Practical Tips for Model Evaluation:

Utilize a Diverse Dataset: Ensure that the evaluation dataset covers a wide range of scenarios and challenges.

Consider Multiple Metrics: Use a combination of metrics to get a comprehensive evaluation.

Regularly Evaluate: Monitor the model's performance over time and retrain as needed.

Use Human Evaluation: Involve human experts to assess the quality of generated text or translations.

Experiment with Different Hyperparameters: Fine-tune hyperparameters like learning rate, batch size, and number of epochs to optimize performance.

Analyze Error Analysis: Identify patterns in the model's mistakes to improve future training.

By effectively evaluating language models, you can gain valuable insights into their strengths and weaknesses, leading to the development of more accurate and robust models.

Chapter 4

Advanced Language Models: Transformers

4.1 The Transformer Architecture Explained

The Transformer architecture has revolutionized the field of natural language processing (NLP) due to its ability to capture long-range dependencies in text sequences. Unlike recurrent neural networks (RNNs), Transformers do not process sequences sequentially, making them more efficient and powerful.

Key Components of a Transformer:

Encoder-Decoder Architecture:

Encoder: Processes the input sequence and generates contextual representations for each token.

Decoder: Generates the output sequence, conditioned on the encoder's output and its own previous outputs.

Self-Attention Mechanism:

Query, Key, and Value: For each token, the model calculates three vectors: query, key, and value.

Attention Scores: The query vector is compared to the key vectors of all tokens in the sequence, and attention scores are calculated.

Weighted Sum: The attention scores are used to weigh the value vectors, resulting in a context-aware representation for the current token.

Positional Encoding:

Since Transformers do not process sequences sequentially, positional encoding is added to the input embeddings to provide information about the relative or absolute position of tokens.

How Transformers Work:

Input Embedding: The input sequence is converted into a sequence of embeddings, which are numerical representations of words or tokens.

Positional Encoding: Positional encoding is added to the input embeddings to provide information about the relative or absolute position of tokens.

Encoder: The input sequence is processed by multiple layers of self-attention and feed-forward neural networks. Each layer captures different levels of contextual information.

Decoder: The decoder generates the output sequence, one token at a time. It uses self-attention to focus on relevant parts of the input sequence and its own previous outputs.

Output: The final output is generated by a linear layer and a softmax function.

Advantages of Transformers:

Parallel Processing: Transformers can process input sequences in parallel, making them more efficient than RNNs.

Long-Range Dependencies: The self-attention mechanism allows Transformers to capture long-range dependencies in text, which is crucial for tasks like machine translation and text summarization.

Strong Performance: Transformers have achieved state-of-the-art results on various NLP tasks, including text classification, question answering, and text generation.

By understanding the Transformer architecture, you can appreciate its power and potential to revolutionize the field of NLP.

4.2 Attention Mechanism: The Heart of Transformers

The attention mechanism is a key component of Transformer models, enabling them to weigh the importance of different parts of the input sequence when processing a specific token. This allows Transformers to capture long-range dependencies in text, which is crucial for tasks like machine translation and text summarization.

How Attention Works:

Query, Key, and Value: For each token in the input sequence, three vectors are calculated:

Query: Represents the current token.

Key: Represents the context of other tokens.

Value: Contains the information associated with each token.

Attention Scores: The query vector is compared to the key vectors of all tokens in the sequence using a dot product or similar operation. The resulting scores indicate how relevant each token is to the current query.

Softmax: The attention scores are normalized using a softmax function to obtain attention weights.

Weighted Sum: The attention weights are used to weigh the value vectors, resulting in a context-aware representation for the current token.

Types of Attention:

Self-Attention: The query, key, and value vectors are derived from the same input sequence. This allows the model to attend to different parts of the input sequence to better understand its context.

Encoder-Decoder Attention: The query vectors are derived from the decoder's previous output, while the key and value vectors are derived from the encoder's output. This allows the decoder to attend to relevant parts of the input sequence when generating the output sequence.

Benefits of Attention:

Long-Range Dependencies: Attention mechanisms can capture long-range dependencies in text, making Transformers suitable for tasks that require understanding the global context.

Interpretability: Attention weights can be visualized to understand how the model focuses on different parts of the input sequence.

Flexibility: Attention can be applied to various NLP tasks, including machine translation, text summarization, question answering, and text generation.

By understanding the attention mechanism, you can appreciate how Transformers achieve state-of-the-art performance on a wide range of NLP tasks.

4.3 Implementing Transformers with Hugging Face

Hugging Face is a popular platform that provides a user-friendly interface and powerful tools for working with state-of-the-art Transformer models. It simplifies the process of fine-tuning pre-trained models and building custom language models.

Key Steps:

Install Hugging Face Transformers:

Bash

```
pip install transformers
```

Load a Pre-trained Model:

Python

```
from transformers import AutoModelForSeq2SeqLM

model_name = "t5-base"
model                                    =
AutoModelForSeq2SeqLM.from_pretrained(model_name)
```

Tokenization:

Python

```python
from transformers import AutoTokenizer

tokenizer = AutoTokenizer.from_pretrained(model_name)

inputs = tokenizer("Hello, world!", return_tensors="pt")
```

Fine-Tuning (Optional):

Prepare a Dataset: Create a dataset of input-output pairs.

Define a Training Loop: Use a training loop to iterate over the dataset, feed data to the model, compute loss, and update model parameters.

Utilize Hugging Face's Trainer API: This provides a convenient way to train models with built-in features like gradient accumulation, early stopping, and logging.

Generate Text:

Python

```python
outputs = model.generate(**inputs)
print(tokenizer.decode(outputs[0],
skip_special_tokens=True))
```

Example: Text Summarization

Python

```python
from transformers import pipeline

summarizer = pipeline("summarization")

text = """
... (Your long text)
"""

summary = summarizer(text)
print(summary[0]['summary_text'])
```

Key Benefits of Using Hugging Face:

Pre-trained Models: Access to a wide range of pre-trained models for various NLP tasks.

Easy Fine-Tuning: Simple APIs for fine-tuning models on custom datasets.

Tokenization: Built-in tokenizers for different languages and tasks.

Model Hub: Share and discover models and datasets.

Community and Support: A large and active community for help and collaboration.

By leveraging Hugging Face, you can quickly and efficiently build and deploy powerful language models for a variety of applications.

Chapter 5

Fine-Tuning Pre-trained Language Models

5.1 Transfer Learning for Language Models

Transfer learning is a technique that leverages knowledge gained from one task to improve performance on a related task. In the context of language models, it involves training a model on a large, general-purpose dataset and then fine-tuning it on a specific task.

Why Transfer Learning?

Reduced Training Time: Pre-trained models have already learned valuable representations, reducing the need for extensive training on specific tasks.

Improved Performance: Leveraging pre-trained models often leads to better performance, especially when working with limited data.

Reduced Data Requirements: Pre-trained models can be fine-tuned on smaller datasets, making them suitable for various applications.

Steps Involved in Transfer Learning:

Pre-training:

Train a large language model on a massive text corpus.

The model learns general language representations, such as word embeddings and syntactic patterns.

Task-Specific Fine-tuning:

Freeze the pre-trained model's weights.

Add task-specific layers, such as a classification layer or a sequence-to-sequence layer.

Train the added layers on the target task's dataset.

Optionally, fine-tune the pre-trained layers to further improve performance.

Popular Pre-trained Language Models:

BERT (Bidirectional Encoder Representations from Transformers): A powerful model for various NLP tasks, including text classification, question answering, and text generation.

GPT-3 (Generative Pre-trained Transformer 3): A large language model capable of generating human-quality text, translating languages, and writing different kinds of creative content.

RoBERTa (Robustly Optimized BERT Pretraining Approach): A more robust version of BERT, trained on a larger dataset and with more training steps.

Advantages of Transfer Learning:

Faster Training: Reduced training time due to pre-trained weights.

Better Performance: Improved performance, especially on smaller datasets.

Broader Applications: Pre-trained models can be adapted to various NLP tasks.

By leveraging transfer learning, you can build powerful language models that achieve state-of-the-art performance on a wide range of tasks, even with limited data.

5.2 Fine-Tuning for Text Generation

Fine-tuning a pre-trained language model for text generation involves adapting the model to a specific text generation task, such as generating creative text formats like poetry or code.

Key Steps in Fine-Tuning:

Prepare a Dataset:

Data Collection: Gather a dataset of text examples that align with the desired generation style or task.

Data Formatting: Format the data into appropriate input-output pairs.

Data Preprocessing: Tokenize the text and convert it into a suitable format for the model.

Choose a Pre-trained Model:

Select a pre-trained language model that is suitable for the task. Popular choices include GPT-2, GPT-3, and T5.

Set Up the Fine-Tuning Process:

Loss Function: Use a cross-entropy loss function to measure the difference between the model's predicted output and the ground truth.

Optimizer: Choose an optimizer like Adam or SGD to update the model's parameters.

Learning Rate: Adjust the learning rate to control the speed of learning.

Train the Model:

Feed the training data into the model.

Calculate the loss.

Update the model's parameters using backpropagation.

Iterate over the training data multiple times (epochs).

Evaluate the Model:

Use metrics like perplexity, BLEU, and ROUGE to evaluate the quality of the generated text.

Analyze the generated text qualitatively to assess its coherence, creativity, and relevance.

Tips for Effective Fine-Tuning:

Start with a Strong Pre-trained Model: A well-trained pre-trained model can significantly improve the performance of the fine-tuned model.

Use a Sufficient Amount of High-Quality Data: A larger and more diverse dataset can lead to better results.

Experiment with Different Hyperparameters: Fine-tune hyperparameters like learning rate, batch size, and number of epochs to optimize performance.

Regularly Evaluate the Model: Monitor the model's performance during training and adjust the training process as needed.

Consider Data Augmentation Techniques: Augment the training data to increase its diversity and improve generalization.

Utilize Regularization Techniques: Prevent overfitting by using techniques like dropout and early stopping.

By following these steps and tips, you can effectively fine-tune language models for a variety of text generation tasks, from creative writing to code generation.

5.3 Fine-Tuning for Text Classification

Fine-tuning a pre-trained language model for text classification involves adapting the model to a specific classification task, such as sentiment analysis, topic classification, or intent recognition.

Key Steps in Fine-Tuning:

Prepare a Dataset:

Data Collection: Gather a dataset of text documents with corresponding labels.

Data Preprocessing: Clean the text data, tokenize it, and convert it into a suitable format for the model.

Data Splitting: Divide the dataset into training, validation, and testing sets.

Choose a Pre-trained Model:

Select a pre-trained language model that is suitable for the task. Popular choices include BERT, RoBERTa, and XLNet.

Set Up the Fine-Tuning Process:

Freeze the Pre-trained Layers: Initially, keep the weights of the pre-trained layers fixed to prevent overfitting.

Add a Classification Layer: Add a classification layer on top of the pre-trained model to output class probabilities.

Loss Function: Use a cross-entropy loss function to measure the difference between the model's predicted probabilities and the true labels.

Optimizer: Choose an optimizer like Adam or SGD to update the parameters of the added classification layer.

Train the Model:

Feed the training data into the model.

Calculate the loss.

Update the parameters of the classification layer using backpropagation.

Iterate over the training data multiple times (epochs).

Evaluate the Model:

Use metrics like accuracy, precision, recall, and F1-score to evaluate the model's performance on the validation and test sets.

Analyze the model's predictions to identify areas for improvement.

Tips for Effective Fine-Tuning:

Start with a Strong Pre-trained Model: A well-trained pre-trained model can significantly improve the performance of the fine-tuned model.

Use a Sufficient Amount of High-Quality Data: A larger and more diverse dataset can lead to better results.

Experiment with Different Hyperparameters: Fine-tune hyperparameters like learning rate, batch size, and number of epochs to optimize performance.

Regularly Evaluate the Model: Monitor the model's performance during training and adjust the training process as needed.

Consider Data Augmentation Techniques: Augment the training data to increase its diversity and improve generalization.

Utilize Regularization Techniques: Prevent overfitting by using techniques like dropout and early stopping.

By following these steps and tips, you can effectively fine-tune language models for a variety of text classification tasks, such as sentiment analysis, topic classification, and intent recognition.

Chapter 6

Text Generation with Language Models

6.1 Generating Text with Language Models

Language models, especially those based on the Transformer architecture, have revolutionized the field of text generation. These models can generate human-quality text, translate languages, write different kinds of creative content, and more.

Here's a step-by-step guide to generating text using a language model:

Choose a Pre-trained Model:

Select a pre-trained language model that suits your needs. Popular options include GPT-3, GPT-2, and T5.

Consider the model's size, training data, and capabilities.

1 Prepare the Input Prompt:

Provide a clear and concise prompt to guide the model's generation.

The prompt can be a single word, a sentence, or a paragraph.

For more creative text generation, experiment with different prompts and styles.

2 Set Generation Parameters:

Temperature: Controls the randomness of the generated text. Higher temperature leads to more creative and diverse outputs, while lower temperature results in more focused and predictable text.

Top-k Sampling: Limits the vocabulary to the top-k most probable tokens at each step.

Top-p Sampling: Samples from the top-p% most probable tokens, where p is a probability threshold.

3 Generate Text:

Feed the input prompt and generation parameters to the model.

The model will generate text token by token, conditioned on the previous tokens and the input prompt.

Continue the generation process until the desired length or a specific stop condition is reached.

4 Post-Processing (Optional):

If necessary, apply post-processing techniques like filtering, editing, or refining the generated text.

This may involve removing repetitive phrases, correcting grammatical errors, or improving the overall coherence.

Example:

Python

```python
from transformers import pipeline

# Load a pre-trained text generation model
generator = pipeline("text-generation", model="gpt2")

# Generate text with a given prompt
prompt = "Write a poem about a lonely robot exploring a distant planet."
output = generator(prompt, max_length=50, num_return_sequences=1)
print(output[0]['generated_text'])
```

Tips for Effective Text Generation:

Experiment with Different Prompts: Try different prompts to explore various creative directions.

Fine-Tune the Model: Train the model on specific datasets to improve its performance on particular tasks.

Use Different Generation Techniques: Experiment with different sampling techniques to control the diversity and quality of the generated text.

Post-Process the Output: Apply editing and refinement techniques to improve the overall quality of the generated text.

Iterate and Refine: Continuously iterate on the generation process to achieve the desired results.

By following these steps and considering the tips, you can effectively use language models to generate creative and informative text.

6.2 Controlling Text Generation: Temperature, Top-k, and Top-p Sampling

When generating text with language models, it's often desirable to control the creativity and coherence of the output. Techniques like temperature, top-k sampling, and top-p sampling can be used to fine-tune the generation process.

Temperature

Temperature is a hyperparameter that controls the randomness of the model's predictions. A higher temperature leads to more diverse and creative outputs, while a lower temperature results in more focused and predictable text.

High Temperature: The model is more likely to explore different possibilities, leading to unexpected and sometimes nonsensical outputs.

Low Temperature: The model is more likely to stick to the most probable choices, resulting in more coherent and predictable text.

Top-k Sampling

Top-k sampling involves selecting the top-k most probable tokens at each generation step. This technique can help to reduce the generation of nonsensical or irrelevant text.

Higher k: More diverse outputs, but also more potential for off-topic or nonsensical text.

Lower k: More focused and coherent outputs, but less creative and diverse.

Top-p Sampling (Nucleus Sampling)

Top-p sampling, also known as nucleus sampling, involves selecting tokens until their cumulative probability exceeds a threshold p. This technique can balance diversity and focus, allowing for more creative and coherent generations.

Higher p: More diverse outputs, similar to higher values of k.

Lower p: More focused and coherent outputs, similar to lower values of k.

Combining Techniques: Often, a combination of these techniques is used to achieve the desired level of creativity and coherence. For example, you might use a low temperature with top-k sampling to generate focused and coherent text, or a higher temperature with top-p sampling to generate more diverse and creative text.

By understanding and effectively using these techniques, you can fine-tune the generation process to achieve your specific goals.

6.3 Creative Text Generation: Poetry, Code, and Scripts

Language models have the potential to generate creative text formats like poetry, code, and scripts. By fine-tuning models on specific datasets and using appropriate techniques, we can unlock their creative potential.

Poetry Generation

To generate poetry, we need to provide the model with a prompt or a specific poetic form (e.g., sonnet, haiku). The model can then generate verses that rhyme, follow a particular meter, or convey a specific emotion.

Key Techniques:

Prompt Engineering: Provide clear and concise prompts to guide the model's creativity.

Temperature Tuning: Adjust the temperature to control the randomness of the generated text.

Fine-Tuning on Poetic Datasets: Train the model on a dataset of poems to improve its poetic abilities.

Code Generation

Language models can generate code snippets or even complete functions. This can be useful for automating tasks, debugging code, or learning new programming languages.

Key Techniques:

Prompt Engineering: Provide specific code prompts or requirements.

Fine-Tuning on Code Datasets: Train the model on large code datasets to improve its code generation capabilities.

Constraint-Based Generation: Use constraints to guide the generation process, such as enforcing syntax rules and semantic correctness.

Script Generation

Language models can generate scripts for movies, plays, or video games. By providing a prompt or a specific genre, the model can generate dialogue, plotlines, and character descriptions.

Key Techniques:

Prompt Engineering: Provide a clear plot summary, character descriptions, or dialogue prompts.

Fine-Tuning on Script Datasets: Train the model on a dataset of scripts to learn the structure and style of different genres.

Character-Based Generation: Generate text character by character, allowing for more control over the style and tone.

Challenges and Considerations:

Quality Control: Ensuring the quality and coherence of generated text requires careful fine-tuning and evaluation.

Ethical Implications: Generating harmful or misleading content is a concern, and ethical guidelines must be followed.

Copyright and Intellectual Property: Generating text that infringes on copyright or intellectual property rights is a legal issue.

By addressing these challenges and leveraging the power of language models, we can unlock their creative potential and generate innovative and inspiring text formats.

Chapter 7

Text Summarization

7.1 Extractive Summarization Techniques

Extractive summarization is a technique that involves identifying and extracting the most important sentences from a document to create a summary. This approach is often used when dealing with factual text, where the key information is explicitly stated.

Common Techniques for Extractive Summarization:

1 Frequency-Based Methods:

Term Frequency-Inverse Document Frequency (TF-IDF): Identifies important words and phrases based on their frequency in the document and their rarity across a larger corpus.

Sentence Length: Longer sentences are often considered more important.

2 Statistical Methods:

Lexical Chain Analysis: Identifies semantic relationships between words and phrases.

TextRank: A graph-based ranking algorithm that assigns importance scores to sentences based on their connections.

3 Machine Learning-Based Methods:

Classification-Based: Treats sentence extraction as a binary classification problem, where each sentence is classified as important or not.

Sequence-to-Sequence Models: Uses neural network models to generate summaries directly from the input text.

Challenges in Extractive Summarization:

Subjectivity: Determining the importance of a sentence can be subjective, and different people may have different opinions.

Contextual Understanding: Understanding the context of a sentence is crucial for accurate summarization, but it can be challenging for machine learning models.

Preserving Coherence: Extracted sentences need to be coherent and flow smoothly to form a meaningful summary.

Improving Extractive Summarization:

Contextual Understanding: Using advanced language models that can understand the context of sentences.

Sentence Ranking: Developing more accurate sentence ranking algorithms to identify the most important information.

Post-Processing: Applying techniques like sentence fusion and reordering to improve the coherence and readability of the summary.

By addressing these challenges and leveraging advanced techniques, we can improve the quality of extractive summarization and create more informative and concise summaries.

7.2 Abstractive Summarization Techniques

Abstractive summarization is a more advanced technique that involves generating new text that captures the key ideas of the original document. Unlike extractive summarization, which selects sentences from the original text, abstractive summarization generates new sentences that may not be directly present in the original text.

Common Techniques for Abstractive Summarization:

1 Sequence-to-Sequence Models:

Encoder-Decoder Architecture: The encoder processes the input text, and the decoder generates the summary, one token at a time.

Attention Mechanism: Helps the model focus on relevant parts of the input sequence when generating the output.

2 Transformer-Based Models:

Self-Attention: Allows the model to weigh the importance of different parts of the input sequence.

Cross-Attention: Enables the decoder to attend to relevant parts of the encoder's output.

3 Reinforcement Learning:

Trains the model to generate summaries that are both informative and fluent.

A reward function is used to evaluate the quality of the generated summaries.

Challenges in Abstractive Summarization:

Factuality: Ensuring that the generated summary is accurate and does not introduce any false information.

Coherence: Maintaining coherence and fluency in the generated text.

Novelty: Generating summaries that are informative but not overly repetitive.

Improving Abstractive Summarization:

Large Language Models: Training models on massive datasets can improve their ability to generate coherent and informative summaries.

Fine-Tuning: Fine-tuning pre-trained models on specific domains or tasks can further enhance performance.

Evaluation Metrics: Developing more sophisticated evaluation metrics that can assess the quality of generated summaries.

By addressing these challenges and leveraging advanced techniques, we can create more sophisticated and informative summaries that capture the essence of the original text.

7.3 Evaluating Summarization Models

Evaluating the quality of generated summaries is crucial to assess the effectiveness of summarization models. Various metrics can be used to evaluate both extractive and abstractive summarization models.

Common Evaluation Metrics:

1 ROUGE (Recall-Oriented Understudy for Gisting Evaluation):

ROUGE-N: Measures the n-gram overlap between the generated summary and the reference summary.

ROUGE-L: Measures the longest common subsequence between the generated summary and the reference summary.

2 METEOR (Metric for Evaluation of Translation with Explicit Ordering):

Considers word-level matching, stemming, and synonymy.

It's more robust than ROUGE and can handle variations in word order and paraphrasing.

3 BERTScore:

Uses pre-trained language models to measure semantic similarity between the generated and reference summaries.

It's more sensitive to semantic meaning and can capture nuances that other metrics may miss.

Challenges in Evaluation:

Subjectivity: Human evaluation is often subjective, and different people may have different opinions about the quality of a summary.

Reference Summaries: Creating high-quality reference summaries can be time-consuming and expensive.

Multiple Reference Summaries: A single document may have multiple valid summaries, making evaluation more challenging.

Improving Evaluation:

Automatic Metrics: Continuously improving automatic metrics to better align with human judgment.

Human Evaluation: Incorporating human evaluation to assess factors like fluency, coherence, and factuality.

Multi-dimensional Evaluation: Considering multiple aspects of the summary, such as informativeness, coherence, and conciseness.

By using a combination of automatic and human evaluation, we can obtain a more accurate assessment of summarization model performance.

Chapter 8

Machine Translation

8.1 Sequence-to-Sequence Models for Translation

Sequence-to-sequence (seq2seq) models are a type of neural network architecture that can be used for various sequence-to-sequence tasks, including machine translation.

How Seq2Seq Models Work:

1 Encoder:

Processes the input sequence (source language) one token at a time.

Encodes the input sequence into a fixed-length vector, known as the context vector.

2 Decoder:

Generates the output sequence (target language) one token at a time.

At each time step, the decoder attends to the context vector and its own previous outputs to generate the next token.

Challenges and Improvements:

Long-Term Dependencies: Traditional seq2seq models can struggle to capture long-range dependencies in the input sequence.

Attention Mechanism: The attention mechanism allows the decoder to focus on relevant parts of the input sequence, improving the model's ability to handle long-range dependencies.

Popular Seq2Seq Models for Translation:

Transformer: A powerful architecture that leverages self-attention to capture long-range dependencies.

RNN-based Models: Recurrent Neural Networks, such as LSTM and GRU, can capture sequential information but may struggle with long sequences.

Improving Translation Quality:

Data Quality and Quantity: High-quality and large-scale parallel corpora are essential for training effective translation models.

Model Architecture: Experimenting with different architectures, such as Transformer-based models, can improve translation quality.

Training Techniques: Techniques like regularization, dropout, and early stopping can help prevent overfitting and improve generalization.

Evaluation Metrics: Using appropriate evaluation metrics, such as BLEU, METEOR, and TER, can help assess the quality of translations.

By addressing these challenges and leveraging advanced techniques, we can develop more accurate and fluent machine translation systems.

8.2 Neural Machine Translation

Neural Machine Translation (NMT) is a state-of-the-art technique that utilizes deep learning models to translate text from one language to another. Unlike traditional statistical machine translation (SMT) methods, NMT treats translation as a single sequence-to-sequence task, allowing for more fluent and contextually accurate translations.

Key Components of NMT:

1 Encoder:

Processes the input sentence (source language) and encodes it into a sequence of vectors.

The encoder can be an RNN, LSTM, or Transformer.

2 Decoder:

Generates the output sentence (target language) one token at a time.

The decoder uses the encoder's output and its own previous outputs to predict the next token.

3 Attention Mechanism:

Allows the decoder to focus on relevant parts of the input sequence when generating the output.

This helps to capture long-range dependencies and improve translation quality.

Advantages of NMT:

Improved Translation Quality: NMT models can produce more fluent and accurate translations compared to SMT.

Contextual Understanding: NMT models can capture contextual information, leading to more accurate translations.

Flexibility: NMT models can be applied to various language pairs and domains.

Challenges and Future Directions:

Data Scarcity: For low-resource languages, it can be challenging to obtain sufficient training data.

Domain Adaptation: NMT models may struggle to translate text from domains that are not well-represented in the training data.

Evaluation Metrics: Developing reliable evaluation metrics for NMT is an ongoing challenge.

Future Directions:

Unsupervised and Semi-Supervised Learning: Reducing reliance on large parallel corpora.

Multi-Task Learning: Training models on multiple tasks simultaneously to improve performance.

Domain Adaptation: Developing techniques to adapt models to specific domains.

By addressing these challenges and exploring new techniques, NMT has the potential to revolutionize machine translation and facilitate cross-cultural communication.

Would you like to delve deeper into a specific aspect of NMT, such as attention mechanisms, evaluation metrics, or training techniques?

8.3 Evaluating Translation Models

Evaluating the quality of machine translation models is crucial to assess their performance and identify areas for improvement. Several metrics and techniques are used to evaluate translation quality:

Automatic Metrics

BLEU (Bilingual Evaluation Understudy): Measures the precision of n-gram matches between the generated translation and reference translations.

METEOR (Metric for Evaluation of Translation with Explicit Ordering): Considers word-level matching, stemming, and synonymy.

TER (Translation Error Rate): Measures the number of editing operations (insertions, deletions, substitutions) required to transform the generated translation into a reference translation.

NIST (National Institute of Standards and Technology): Similar to BLEU but considers more complex n-gram matching.

Human Evaluation

Direct Assessment: Human evaluators compare the generated translations to reference translations and assign scores based on fluency, accuracy, and adequacy.

Indirect Assessment: Human evaluators perform tasks like summarization or question answering using the translations and assess the quality based on the results.

Challenges in Evaluation:

Subjectivity: Human evaluation can be subjective, and different evaluators may have different opinions.

Reference Quality: The quality of reference translations can impact the evaluation results.

Domain-Specific Evaluation: Different domains may require specific evaluation metrics and techniques.

Improving Evaluation:

Multiple Metrics: Combining multiple metrics can provide a more comprehensive evaluation.

Human-in-the-Loop Evaluation: Incorporating human feedback can help identify biases and errors in automatic metrics.

Domain-Specific Evaluation: Developing domain-specific evaluation metrics and datasets.

Contextual Understanding: Evaluating the translation in context, considering the source and target languages, and the specific task.

By carefully evaluating translation models, researchers and developers can identify areas for improvement and develop more accurate and fluent translation systems.

Chapter 9

Question Answering Systems

9.1 Reading Comprehension Tasks

Reading comprehension tasks involve understanding and answering questions about a given text. These tasks are essential in natural language processing, as they test a model's ability to understand the meaning and context of text.

Common Reading Comprehension Tasks:

1 Question Answering:

Given a question and a passage of text, the model must identify the relevant information and provide a concise answer.

Example: "What is the capital of France?" given a passage about French history and geography.

2 Text Summarization:

Given a text document, the model must generate a shorter summary that captures the main ideas.

Example: Summarizing a news article or a research paper.

3 Textual Entailment:

Given a pair of sentences (premise and hypothesis), the model must determine whether the hypothesis logically follows from the premise.

Example: "Premise: The sky is blue. Hypothesis: The sky is not green."

4 Coreference Resolution:

Given a text, the model must identify which words or phrases refer to the same entity.

Example: Identifying that "he" and "the president" refer to the same person in a news article.

Challenges in Reading Comprehension:

Contextual Understanding: Understanding the context of a word or phrase can be challenging, especially in ambiguous or complex sentences.

World Knowledge: Models need to access and utilize world knowledge to answer questions that require common sense or background information.

Long-Range Dependencies: Capturing long-range dependencies between words and phrases is crucial for understanding complex text.

Approaches to Reading Comprehension:

Traditional Methods: Rule-based systems and statistical methods.

Machine Learning Methods: Support Vector Machines (SVM), Naive Bayes, and Random Forests.

Deep Learning Methods: Recurrent Neural Networks (RNNs), Long Short-Term Memory (LSTM) networks, and Transformer-based models.

By addressing these challenges and leveraging advanced techniques, we can develop more powerful reading comprehension models that can understand and reason about text.

9.2 Extractive Question Answering

Extractive question answering is a technique that involves identifying and extracting the most relevant spans of text from a given passage to answer a specific question.

Key Steps in Extractive Question Answering:

1 Question Understanding:

The model processes the question to understand its intent and identify key keywords.

2 Passage Understanding:

The model processes the passage to understand its meaning and identify relevant information.

3 Answer Extraction:

The model identifies the span of text in the passage that best answers the question.

This can be done using techniques like attention mechanisms or pointer networks.

Challenges in Extractive Question Answering:

Contextual Understanding: The model must be able to understand the context of the question and the passage to identify the correct answer.

Long-Range Dependencies: The model may need to capture long-range dependencies between words and phrases to understand the meaning of the passage.

Ambiguity: Questions and passages can be ambiguous, leading to multiple possible answers.

Approaches to Extractive Question Answering:

Traditional Methods: Rule-based systems and statistical methods.

Machine Learning Methods: Support Vector Machines (SVM), Naive Bayes, and Random Forests.

Deep Learning Methods: Recurrent Neural Networks (RNNs), Long Short-Term Memory (LSTM) networks, and Transformer-based models.

Evaluation Metrics:

Exact Match (EM): Measures the percentage of questions answered exactly correctly.

F1-score: Measures the harmonic mean of precision and recall.

By addressing these challenges and leveraging advanced techniques, we can develop more accurate and robust extractive question answering systems.

9.3 Generative Question Answering

Generative question answering is a more advanced technique that involves generating a natural language answer to a given question, rather than simply extracting text from the passage. This allows for more flexible and informative responses.

Key Steps in Generative Question Answering:

1 Question Understanding:

The model processes the question to understand its intent and identify key keywords.

2 Passage Understanding:

The model processes the passage to understand its meaning and identify relevant information.

3 Answer Generation:

The model generates a natural language answer that addresses the question, leveraging the information from the passage.

This can be done using techniques like sequence-to-sequence models or language models.

Challenges in Generative Question Answering:

Factuality: Ensuring that the generated answer is accurate and consistent with the information in the passage.

Coherence: Generating text that is coherent and grammatically correct.

Relevance: Ensuring that the generated answer is relevant to the question and the passage.

Approaches to Generative Question Answering:

Sequence-to-Sequence Models: These models can be used to generate text directly from the input question and passage.

Language Models: Large language models, such as GPT-3, can be used to generate text that is coherent and relevant to the question.

Evaluation Metrics:

BLEU: Measures the similarity between the generated answer and reference answers.

ROUGE: Measures the overlap between the generated answer and reference answers.

METEOR: Measures the semantic similarity between the generated answer and reference answers.

Human Evaluation: Human evaluators can assess the quality of the generated answers based on factors like fluency, relevance, and factuality.

By addressing these challenges and leveraging advanced techniques, we can develop more sophisticated generative question answering systems that can provide more informative and comprehensive answers.

Chapter 10

Ethical Considerations in Language Model Development

10.1 Bias and Fairness in Language Models

Language models, while powerful, can inadvertently perpetuate biases present in the data they are trained on. This can lead to unfair and discriminatory outcomes, particularly for marginalized groups.[1]

Sources of Bias:

Biased Training Data: If the training data is biased, the model will learn to replicate those biases.

Algorithmic Bias: Certain algorithms may inherently amplify biases present in the data.

Societal Biases: The model may reflect societal biases that are encoded in language and culture.

Types of Bias:

Representational Bias: The model may underrepresent or misrepresent certain groups.

Algorithmic Bias: The model's algorithms may favor certain groups over others.

Amplification Bias: The model may amplify existing biases in the data.

Mitigating Bias:

Fairness-Aware Training: Incorporating fairness constraints into the training process.

Data Debiasing: Identifying and mitigating biases in the training data.

Model Auditing: Regularly auditing the model's outputs to identify and address biases.

User-Centric Design: Designing models that are transparent and accountable to users.

Challenges in Mitigating Bias:

Identifying Bias: It can be difficult to identify all sources of bias in a complex model.

Balancing Fairness and Accuracy: Mitigating bias can sometimes come at the cost of accuracy.

Evolving Nature of Bias: Biases can emerge over time as language and society evolve.

By understanding the sources and types of bias, and by employing effective mitigation techniques, we can develop language models that are fair, unbiased, and beneficial to all.

10.2 Privacy and Security Concerns in Language Models

As language models become more powerful and widely used, concerns about privacy and security have grown. Here are some key issues to consider:

Privacy Concerns

Data Privacy: Language models are trained on massive amounts of text data. This data may contain sensitive personal information, raising concerns about privacy.

Model Privacy: The model itself can be considered intellectual property, and protecting it from unauthorized access and misuse is important.

Security Concerns

Adversarial Attacks: Malicious actors can manipulate the model's inputs or outputs to produce harmful or misleading results.

Model Theft: Models can be stolen and used for malicious purposes.

Data Poisoning: Malicious actors can introduce biased or harmful data into the training data.

Mitigating Risks

To address these concerns, several strategies can be employed:

Data Privacy:

Anonymization and De-identification: Removing personally identifiable information from the training data.

Differential Privacy: Adding noise to the data to protect individual privacy.

Model Privacy:

Model Watermarking: Embedding a watermark or signature into the model to protect intellectual property.

Model Obfuscation: Making the model more difficult to reverse engineer.

Adversarial Attacks:

Adversarial Training: Training the model on adversarial examples to improve its robustness.

Input Validation: Validating and sanitizing inputs to prevent malicious attacks.

Data Poisoning:

Robust Training Algorithms: Using robust training algorithms that are less susceptible to poisoning attacks.

Data Validation: Carefully validating and cleaning the training data to remove malicious inputs.

By implementing these measures, we can mitigate the risks associated with language models and ensure their safe and responsible use.

10.3 Responsible AI Practices

Responsible AI practices are essential for ensuring that AI systems are developed and deployed ethically and responsibly. These practices aim to mitigate biases, promote fairness, and safeguard privacy.

Key Principles of Responsible AI:

1 Fairness: AI systems should be designed to avoid bias and discrimination, treating all users fairly.

2 Transparency: AI systems should be understandable and explainable, allowing users to understand how decisions are made.

3 Privacy and Security: AI systems should protect user privacy and data security.

4 Accountability: Organizations should be accountable for the development and deployment of AI systems.

5 Robustness and Reliability: AI systems should be reliable and resilient to attacks.

Implementing Responsible AI Practices:

1 Data Quality and Bias:

Data Quality Assurance: Ensure that the data used to train AI models is accurate, complete, and free of errors.

Bias Detection and Mitigation: Identify and mitigate biases in the data and algorithms.

2 Model Interpretability:

Explainable AI: Develop techniques to explain the decision-making process of AI models.

Model Debugging: Identify and fix errors in the model's behavior.

3 Privacy and Security:

Data Privacy: Implement strong data privacy measures, such as encryption and anonymization.

Security: Protect AI systems from cyberattacks and unauthorized access.

4 Ethical Considerations:

Ethical Guidelines: Develop and adhere to ethical guidelines for AI development and deployment.

Human Oversight: Ensure that humans are involved in the development and deployment of AI systems.

Challenges and Future Directions

While there has been significant progress in responsible AI, several challenges remain:

Technical Challenges: Developing robust and unbiased AI models is a complex task.

Ethical Challenges: Defining and implementing ethical guidelines for AI is challenging.

Regulatory Challenges: The regulatory landscape for AI is still evolving.

To address these challenges, ongoing research and collaboration between researchers, policymakers, and industry leaders are crucial. By embracing responsible AI practices, we can harness the power of AI while minimizing its potential harms.